Quick JavaScript Int Questions

Published By

Sandeep Kumar Patel.

Table of Contents

Chapter 1 Inheritance

Q. How to create a class?
ANSWER
JavaScript does not have a class definition. To mimic classes in JavaScript functions can be used to declare a class.

Example:
Let's create a student class in JavaScript which takes two parameters name and roll as property. The code will look like below,

```
function Student(name,roll){
    this.name = name;
    this.roll = roll;
}
```

Q. How to create an object?
ANSWER
An object in JavaScript can be created using two ways:-

New Keyword:
To create a student object from the above student class we can call the Student function using new keyword.

```
var student1  = new Student('sandeep',2)
```

Anonymous Object:
Anonymous objects can be created using pair of curly braces containing property name and value pairs.

```
Var rose = {'color': 'red'}
```

Q. How to declare a private and a public member?

Private members are declared using **var** keyword and constructor function.

```
function Student(name,roll){
    var id= ABCD123;
    this.name = name;
    this.roll = roll;
}
```

When a Student object will be created the propertied name and roll will be accessible using dot operator but **id** will not be accessible as it behaves as a private member and return **undefined** on call.

```
Elements  Resources  Network  Sources  Timeline  Profil
> function Student(name,roll){
        var id= "ABCD123";
        this.name = name;
        this.roll = roll;
    }
    undefined
> var student1 = new Student('sandeep',25)
    undefined
> student1.name
    "sandeep"
> student1.id
    undefined
>
```

The above chrome console is showing a student1 object is created.name property is accessible as it is showing sandeep on student1.name call. So name is a public property for the student object. But id property is not accessible and returned undefined on student1.id call. This shows id is a private property in student1 object.

Q. What is prototype property?

By Using Prototype we can add **new members** to an existing object. Every JavaScript object has this property internally. Initially it is an **empty** object.

Example:

```
function Student(name,roll){
    this.name = name;
    this.roll = roll;
}
var student1 = new Student('sangeeta',30);
Student.prototype.mark = 100;
```

Checkout the below chrome console for the use of protype.

```
Elements   Resources   Network   Sources   Timeline   Profiles
>  function Student(name,roll){
        this.name = name;
        this.roll = roll;
   }
   undefined
>  var student1 = new Student('sangeeta',30)
   undefined
>  student1
   Student {name: "sangeeta", roll: 30}
>  Student.prototype.mark = 100
   100
>  student1
   Student {name: "sangeeta", roll: 30, mark: 100}
>
```

Initially the student1 object has only two properties name and roll. By using prototype a new property **mark** has been added to student object with a value of **100**.Now the console shows that the mark property is also added to the existing **student1** object.

Q. What is constructor property?

ANSWER

Constructor property of an object maintains a reference to its creator function.

Example:

Let us checkout an example by creating a student object and calling the constructor property on it.

```
function Student(name, mark){
    this.name=name;
    this.mark =mark;
}
var student1 = new Student('sandeep',123);
console.log(student1.constructor);
```

Checkout the following screen shot for above code in chrome console. The console log is printing the referenced function by **student1** object.

```
Elements  Resources  Network  Sources  Timeline  Profiles  Audits  Console
> function Student(name,mark){this.name=name; this.mark =mark;}
  undefined
> var student1 = new Student('sandeep',123)
  undefined
> console.log(student1.constructor)
  function Student(name,mark){this.name=name; this.mark =mark;}
< undefined
> |
```

Q. How to call other class methods?

ANSWER

Using **call()** and **apply()** method we can use methods from different context to the current context. It is really helpful in reusability of code and context binding.

- **call()** : It is used to calls a function with a given this value

and arguments provided individually.
- **apply():** It is used to call a function with a given this value and arguments provided as an array.

Below code has two function **getTypeOfNumber()** and **getTypeOfAllNumber().** The details pf these functions are below.
- **getTypeOfNumber** : This method takes single number as parameter and return the type either Even or Odd.
- **getTypeOfAllNumber** : This method takes array of numbers as parameter and return the types in an array with Even or Odd.

```
var MyNumber = {
  getTypeOfNumber : function(number){
    var type = (number % 2 === 0) ? "Even" : "Odd";
    return type;
  },
  getTypeOfAllNumber : function (){
    var result = [],i=0;
    for (; i < arguments.length; i++){
      var type =
MyNumber.getTypeOfNumber.call(null,arguments[i])
;
      result.push(type)
    }
    return result;
  }
};
var typeOfNumber =
MyNumber.getTypeOfNumber.call(null,21)
console.log(typeOfNumber)
var typeOfAllNumber =
MyNumber.getTypeOfAllNumber.apply(null,[2,4,5,7
8,21])
console.log(typeOfAllNumber)
```

Below screenshot shows output of the above code Firebug console.

```
> var MyNumber = {        getTypeOfNumber : function(...ull,[2,4,5,78,21])
  console.log(typeOfAllNumber)

  Odd

  [ "Even", "Even", "Odd", "Even", "Odd" ]
```

Q. Explain method overriding with an Example?
ANSWER

We can override any inbuilt method of JavaScript by declaring its definition again. The existing definition is accessible to override by the **prototype** property. Consider the below example, **split()** is an built-in method for a string object .Its default behaviour to break the specified string to an array and is a member function of **String** class. But we have overridden its definition using its prototype property.

Below screenshot shows the inbuilt behaviour of **split()** method. It has divided the string into an array of element.

```
> var output1 = 'elephant'.split('e');    1  var output1 = 'elephant'.split('e');
  console.log('before overiding : ',      2
  output1);                               3  console.log('before overiding : ', output1);
  before overiding : [ "", "l", "phant" ] 4
```

The following screenshot shows the new overridden definition of **split ()** method. It is now normally returns string **"I am overriden"**.

```
> var output1 = 'elephant'.split('e');    1
  console.log('before overiding : ',      2  String.prototype.split = function(param){
  output1);                               3
                                          4     return "I am overriden";
  before overiding : [ "", "l", "phant" ] 5
> String.prototype.split =               6  }
  function(param){    ...");             7
  console.log("after overiding : ",       8  var output2 = "elephant".split("e");
  output2);                               9
                                         10  console.log("after overiding : ", output2);
  after overiding : I am overriden
```

Q. How to inherit from a class?
ANSWER
Inheritance can be achieved in JavaScript using **prototype** property.

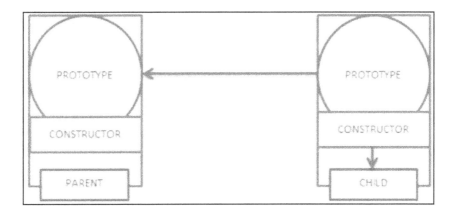

We need to follow 2 steps to create an inheritance.

Step1:
Child class prototype should point to parent class object.

<ChildClassName>.prototype = new <ParentClass>();

Step2:
Reset the child class prototype constructor to point self.

<ChildClassName>.prototype.constructor=<ChildClassName>

Example:
Below example shows **ScienceStudent** class as a child class of **Student** class. As the method **showMyType()** is available for ScienceStudent object.

```
function Student(name){
    this.name=name;
}
Student.prototype.sayMyType = function(){
```

```
    console.log("I am student type")
}
function ScienceStudent(name){
}
ScienceStudent.prototype = new Student();
ScienceStudent.prototype.constructor = ScienceStudent;
var student2 = new ScienceStudent('sangeeta');
console.log(student2.sayMyType());
```

Check out the below screen shot for the output of the above code in the developer console.

```
Elements  Resources  Network  Sources  Timeline  Profiles  Audits
> function Student(name){
      this.name=name;
  }
  Student.prototype.sayMyType = function(){
      console.log("I am student type")
  }
  function ScienceStudent(name){
  }
  ScienceStudent.prototype = new Student();
  ScienceStudent.prototype.constructor = ScienceStudent;
  var student2 = new ScienceStudent('sangeeta');
  console.log(student2.sayMyType());
  I am student type
```

To test the type of an object belongs to a class or not **instanceOf** can be used. This returns a Boolean value, **TRUE** for an object belongs to a class or else **FALSE**. Check the below screen shot for the test of student2 object using **instanceOf**.

Q. What is differential inheritance?

ANSWER

Differential Inheritance is a common prototype-oriented model that uses the concept that most objects are derived from other, more generic objects, and only differ in a few small aspects. Each object maintains a reference to its prototype and a table of properties that are different.

Q. What is Object.create() method do?

ANSWER

ECMAScript 5.1 has this method in its specification. This method can be used to create a new object with given prototype object and properties. The syntax of this method is listed below.

    Object.create(proto[, propertiesObject])

Example:
Below code has a Student class function with name property and the prototype object has a method getStudentName() which return the name of the student. A new student1 object has been creates using Object.create() method by passing the prototype object of Student with value of the name as sandeep. Then the getStudentName() method is called on student1 object and logged in the console.

```
function Student(name) {
  this.name = name;
```

```
    }

    Student.prototype = {
       getStudentName: function() {
          return "Name of Student is :" + this.name;
       }
    };

    var student1 = Object.create(Student.prototype);
    student1.name = "Sandeep";
    console.log(student1.getStudentName());
```

The following screenshot shows the output of the above code in the developer console.

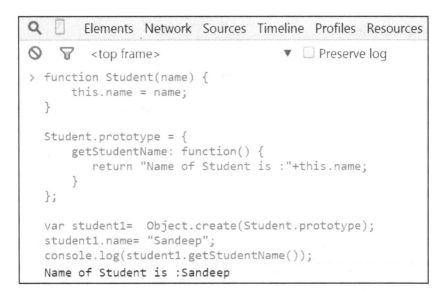

Q. Write a polyfill for Object.create() method if it is not present in the browser?

ANSWER

ECMAScript 5.1 has this method in its specification. If the browser is old then Object.create() method is not present. To resolve this we need to write a polyfill. Below code shows the polyfill for Object.create() method.

```javascript
//check if create method is present inside Object
if (typeof Object.create != 'function') {
    //define the create method
    Object.create = (function() {
        var Object = function() {};

        return function(prototype) {

            if (arguments.length > 1) {
                throw Error('Second argument not supported');
            }

            if (typeof prototype != 'object') {
                throw TypeError('Argument must be an object');
            }

            Object.prototype = prototype;

            var result = new Object();

            Object.prototype = null;

            return result;
        };
    })();
}
```

The above code checks if the create() method is already present inside the Object using if condition and comparing its type to function. If this condition true it means the create() method is not present. Then the polyfill code block gets executes and assigns the empty object to Object.create property.

Q. What is the purpose of Object.defineProperties() method?
ANSWER
ECMAScript 5.1 provides Object.defineProperties() method to create
new properties to a defined object. It provides many configuration
options to initialize these members. Below code shows the use of
this method.

```
function Student(name) {
   this.name = name;
}
var student1 = Object.create(Student.prototype),
properties ={
  "subject": {
  value: "Computer",
  writable: true,
  enumerable:true
 },
  "marks": {
  value: 0,
  writable: false,
  enumerable:true
 }
};
Object.defineProperties(student1, properties);
student1.name = "Sandeep";
student1.subject ="Mathematics";
student1.marks=75;
console.log(student1);
```

In the above code a student1 object created using Object.create()
method. Then some new properties like subject and marks are added
to this object. The enumerable option decided whether the property
can be enumerated as own property. Writable property decides
whether the property is modifiable or not. The value property takes
the default value of the property. Below screenshot shows the
output of the above code in the developer console.

```
        Q           Elements  Network  Sources  Timeline  Profiles  Resources  Audits
        ⊘   ▽    <top frame>                        ▼   ☐ Preserve log
    >  function Student(name) {
            this.name = name;
        }
       var student1 = Object.create(Student.prototype),
       properties ={
          "subject": {
             value: "Computer",
             writable: true,
             enumerable:true
          },
          "marks": {
             value: 0,
             writable: false,
             enumerable:true
          }
       };
       Object.defineProperties(student1, properties);
       student1.name = "Sandeep";
       student1.subject ="Mathematics";
       student1.marks=75;
       console.log(student1);
       Object {subject: "Mathematics", marks: 0, name: "Sandeep"}
```

Q. How can you distinguish scope and context in JavaScript?

ANSWER

Scope pertains to the visibility of variables and context refers to the object to which a method belongs and can be changed by using call or applies.

Q. What are two ways in which the variable can be assigned to an empty object?

ANSWER

When creating a new empty object, you can instantiate the Object() constructor or you can simply create an empty object literal. In either case, you can then add properties to the new object. The syntax of creating empty object is listed below.

```
var aEmptyObject= new Object();
var aEmptyObject= = {};
```

Chapter 2 Questions on Event

Q. How Event works?
ANSWER
Event propagation follows two phases **capturing** and **bubbling** phase.

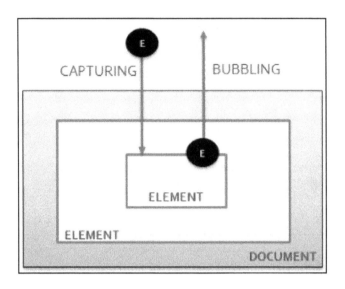

Capturing Phase:
In this phase, event first makes its way **downwards** from the **DOCUMENT** to the **target** element by passing all inner elements.

Bubbling Phase:
In this phase event makes its way back **upwards** from the **target** element to **DOCUMENT** by passing all outer wrapped elements.

Q. How to attach event to an element?
ANSWER
According to DOM Level 2 Event Specification an event can be attached to an element using **addEventListener()** method using **three** arguments.

Syntax:

```
<element>.addEventListener(<eventname>,<eventcallback>,<bo
oleanphase>)
```

eventname:
Represents type of event as String parameter. For Example click, mouseover, mouseout etc.

eventcallback:
This represents the callback function to be called for the event to be handled.

booleanphase :
This represents the phase of the event where the listener is attached. A FALSE value represents the bubbling phase and a TRUE value represents a capturing phase.

Example:
A click event listener is added to the document which alerts a message when click occur.

```
document.addEventListener('click', function () {
    alert("Insider Event Listener");
},false);
```

Q. How to attach event prior to IE9 browser version?
ANSWER
In IE older bowser an event can be attached to an element using attachEvent() method. Only For bubbling phase a listener can be added.

Syntax:
```
<element>.attachEvent(<eventname>,<eventcallback>)
```

Example:
A click event listener is added to the document which alerts a message when click occur. Below screenshot shows adding a click event in IE 10 developer toolbar.

```
HTML    CSS    Console   Script   Profiler   Network

>> document.attachEvent('onclick',function () {
       console.log("Insider Event Listener");
   });
   true
Insider Event Listener


document.attachEvent('onclick',function () {
    console.log("Insider Event Listener");
});
```

Except IE, the other browser added by **addEventListener()** method. Below screenshot shows the demonstration this method in Firebug.

```
Console ▾  HTML  CSS  Script  DOM  Net  Cookies  Page Speed  Typography

Clear  Persist  Profile   All  Err  Run  Clear  Copy  Pretty Print  History
Inside Event Handler Method  1  var handlerMethod = function(e){
                             2       console.log("Inside Event Handler Method");
                             3  }
                             4
                             5  document.addEventListener('click',handlerMethod);
                             6
```

Q. How to remove event listener?

ANSWER

According to DOM Level 2 Event Specification an Event Listener can be removed using **removeEventListener()** method. For IE browsers **detachEvent()** method must be used.

The following screenshot shows detaching click event handler from document for IE browser.

The following screenshot shows removing click event handler from document for Firefox browser.

Q. How setTimeOut() and clearTimeOut() function works?
ANSWER

The **setTimeout()** method calls a function or evaluates an expression **once** after a specified number of milliseconds. **clearTimeOut()** method stop the execution of the function specified in the **setTimeout()** method.

Syntax:
    var timeOut = setTimeout(function,milliseconds,lang)
    clearTimeout(timeOut)

Below code shows the demonstration of these time out methods.

    var timeOutHandler= function(){

```
        console.log("inside Time Now ", new Date().getSeconds());
        clearTimeout(timeOut)
    }
    console.log("Time Now ", new Date().getSeconds());
    var timeOut = setTimeout(timeOutHandler,4000);
```

Below screenshot show the execution of the **timeOutHandler()** method after 4 seconds.

Q. How setInterval() and clearInterval() function works?

ANSWER

The **setInterval()** method calls a function or evaluates an expression in specified **interval** of milliseconds. **clearInterval()** method stop the execution of the function specified in the **setInterval()** method.

Syntax:
```
    var timeInterval = setInterval(function, milliseconds)
    clearInterval(timeInterval)
```

Below code demonstrate these interval handlers.

```
    var counter = 0,
      timeIntervaltHandler= function(){
        console.log("inside Time Now ", new Date().getSeconds());
        counter++;
        console.log("Handler Called count ",counter)
        if(counter === 4) {
          clearInterval(timeInterval);
          console.log("Clearing the interval handler")
        }
```

```
        }
        console.log("Time Now ", new Date().getSeconds());
        var timeInterval = setInterval(timeIntervaltHandler,2000);
```

Below screenshot shows the handler called every 2 second for 4
times .After 4th called **clearInterval()** remove the execution.

```
  ↩ ↩ ‹ › ≣   Console ▾  HTML  CSS  Script  DOM  Net  Cookies  Page Speed  Typography
 ·e   Clear  Persist  Profile  All  Errors   Run  Clear  Copy  Pretty Print  History
var counter = 0,                    1  var counter = 0,
timeIntervaltHandler= funct...erva       timeIntervaltHandler= function(){
setInterval(timeIntervaltHandler,2           console.log("inside Time Now ", new Date().getSeconds());
                                             counter++;
  Time Now 10                                console.log("Handler Called count ",counter)
                                             if(counter === 4) {
  inside Time Now 12                           clearInterval(timeInterval);
                                               console.log("Clearing the interval handler")
  Handler Called count 1                      }
                                          }
  inside Time Now 14                 10 }
                                     11  console.log("Time Now ", new Date().getSeconds());
  Handler Called count 2            11  var timeInterval = setInterval(timeIntervaltHandler,2000);|

  inside Time Now 16

  Handler Called count 3

  inside Time Now 18

  Handler Called count 4

  Clearing the interval handler
```

Chapter 3 Closure

ANSWER
A closure is an inner function that has access to the outer wrapped function's variables. It has three different scope accesses:-
Self-scope:
It has access to properties present in its own scope.
Wrapped function's scope:
It has access to the properties present to from its enclosing function.
Global Scope:
It has access to the properties present in global scope that is window scope.
Example:
The inner function still has the access to prop1 though prop1 belongs to outer function scope.

```
function myOuterFunction(){
    var prop1 = 5;
    return function innerFunction(){
        return prop1;
    }
}
var res = myOuterFunction();
console.log(res.name);
console.log(res());
```

Below screenshot shows the output of the above code in the console.

```
  Elements   Resources   Network   Sources   Timelir
> function myOuterFunction(){
      var prop1 = 5;
      return function innerFunction(){
          return prop1;
      }
  }
  var res = myOuterFunction();
  console.log(res.name);
  console.log(res());
  innerFunction
  5
```

Q. Give an example of practical implication of closure concept?
ANSWER

In web page development closures are more frequently used by the developers. A most common scenario is when we need some kind of factory which will return a function object with different value that can be used by application.

Example:

The following code has a background color factory named backgroundColorFactory which returns a function with an input color. Using this factory we have created greenBackground and blueBackground function objects and binded with the 2 buttons. Once user clicks these buttons the background color of the body is changed to the targeted color.

```
<!DOCTYPE html>
<html>

<head>
  <meta charset="utf-8">
  <title>Practical Closure Example</title>
</head>
```

```
<body>
  <button id="greenButton">Green Background</button>
  <button id="blueButton">Blue Background</button>
  <script>
    var backgroundColorFactory = function(color) {
      return function() {
        document.body.style.background = color;
      };
    };

    var greenBackground = backgroundColorFactory('green');
    var blueBackground = backgroundColorFactory('blue');

    document.getElementById('greenButton').onclick =
greenBackground;
    document.getElementById('blueButton').onclick =
blueBackground;
  </script>
</body>

</html>
```

The output of the above code is listed in below screenshot.

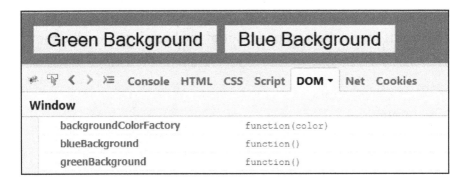

Q. Emulate the private data using closure?
ANSWER
The following code demonstrates the declaration of private variable

_name. It means we can assign the _name value using Student constructor with a new keyword.

```
function Student(name) {
  var _name = name;

  this.getName = function() {
    return _name;
  };
}

var student1 = new Student("Sandeep");
student1._name = "John";
console.log(student1.getName());
```

The details of the previous code are as follows:
- A Student object **student1** is created with **_name** has value **Sandeep**.
- A new name value **John** is assigned to _name but the **getName()** method prints **Sandeep** to the console. It proves _name is private.

The following screenshot shows the Chrome console with the output of the previous code.

Chapter 4 Questions on JSON

Q. What is JSON ?
ANSWER
The JSON text format is syntactically identical to the code for creating JavaScript objects. JSON is only a subset of JS object literal notation, but apart from looking similar, they have nothing in common. JSON is used as data exchange format, like XML.
JSON is built on two structures:

- A collection of name/value pairs. In various languages, this is realized as an object, record, struct, dictionary, hash table, keyed list, or associative array.
- An ordered list of values. In most languages, this is realized as an array, vector, list, or sequence.

Q. Why does Google prepend while (1); to their JSON responses?
ANSWER
It prevents JSON hijacking. This is to ensure some other site can't do nasty tricks to try to steal data. By replacing the array constructor, then including this JSON URL via a <script> tag, a malicious third-party site could steal the data from the JSON response. By putting a while(1); at the start, the script will crash instead. A same-site request using XHR and a separate JSON parser, on the other hand, can easily ignore the while(1); prefix.

Q. What is JSONP ?
ANSWER
JSONP stands for "**JSON with Padding**". It means JSON data wrapped in a function call. A callback (processing/padding) function already defined in the Web page at the time of requesting remote JSON data.

Example:
The below JavaScript code shows a callback function paddingFunction()
for a remote URL
//abcdurl .

```
function paddingFunction(data){
 console.log("response data processing code")
}
var script = document.createElement('script');
script.src = '//abcdurl?callback=paddingFunction'
document.getElementsByTagName('head')[0].appendChild(scrip
t);
```

Q. Why use JSON over XML ?

ANSWER

The following points are in favor of JSON over XML format:

- JSON can contain Integer, String, List, Arrays. XML is just nodes and elements that needs to be parsed into Integer, String and so on before it is used by your application.
- JSON is smaller, faster and lightweight compared to XML. So for data delivery between servers and browsers, JSON is a better choice.
- JSON is best for use of data in web applications from web services because of JavaScript which supports JSON. The overhead of parsing XML nodes is more compare to a quick look up in JSON.
- For a newbie, JSON might look complex to read and understand because of its structure unless it is well written with all brackets and commas properly indented.
- JSON can be mapped more easily into object oriented system.
- JSON and XML both use Unicode and thus support Internationalization.
- JSON is a better data exchange format. XML is a better document exchange format.
- JSON is less secure because of absence of JSON parser in browser.
- If the data is in XML, you can write an XSLT template and run it over the XML to output the data into another format: HTML, SVG, plain text, comma-delimited, even JSON. When

you have data in JSON, it's pretty much stuck there. There's no easy way to change it into another data format. So here, XML scores over JSON.

Q. What is MIME type for JSON?
ANSWER
The MIME type for JSON is **application/json**.

Q. What data types are supported by JSON?
ANSWER
Different data types supported by JSON are Number, String, Boolean, Array, Object, null. The following code shows a JSON object containing different data types:

```
{
    name:"Sandeep",
    score:65,
    isPassed: true,
    subject: ["Computer", "Algebra"],
    address: { city:"Bangalore", country:"India"},
    email: null
}
```

The following screenshot shows the above JSON object in a chrome developer console with all properties listed in key value pair.

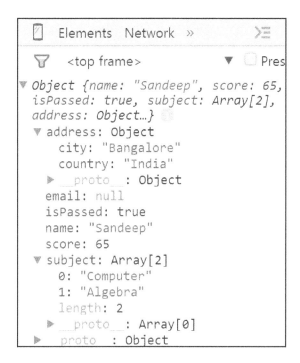

Q. What is the role of JSON.stringify() method?

ANSWER

JSON.stringify() turns an object into a JSON text and stores that JSON text in a string. The following screenshot shows the use of **stringify()** method:

```
Q  🗔  Elements  Network  Sources  Timeline  »              ⋮⋮⋮

⊘  ▽  <top frame>                    ▼ ☐ Preserve log

>   var Student = function(name,score){
            this.name = name;
            this.score = score;
        };
        var student1 = new Student("Sandeep",75);
        console.log(JSON.stringify(student1));
    {"name":"Sandeep","score":75}
```

Q. What is the role of JSON.parse() method?

The **JSON.parse()** method parses a string as JSON, optionally transforming the value produced by parsing. The following screenshot shows the use of **JSON.parse()** method to convert the student1 JSON string to a JSON object.

```
☐ Elements  »                    >☰ ✿ ▢

▽ <top frame>                    ▼ ▢ Pre

var Student = function(name,score)
{
        this.name = name;
        this.score = score;
    };
    var student1 = new
Student("Sandeep",75),
        student1JSONString =
JSON.stringify(student1);

console.log(JSON.parse(student1JSO
NString));
                                 VM52:8
Object {name: "Sandeep", score:
75}
```

Q. What is the complete syntax of JSON.parse() method?

The complete syntax for **JSON.parse()** method is as follows:

```
JSON.parse(text[, reviver])
```

The details of the above syntax are as follows:
- **Text**: It represents the string to parse as JSON.
- **Reviver**: It represents a function, prescribes how the value originally produced by parsing is transformed, before being returned.

Q. How to convert date object to JSON?

The **toJSON()** method can convert the date object to JSON. The following screenshot shows the use of **toJSON()** method for a date object in chrome console.

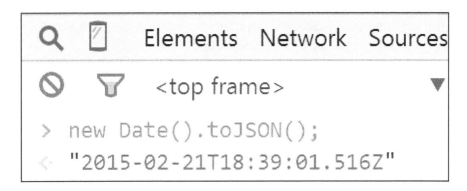

Chapter 5 Questions on DOM

Q. What is DOM ?
ANSWER
Document Object Model (DOM) is a programming API for HTML and XML document. JavaScript is most widely used language to access these DOM API properties and methods.

Q. What are the different objects involved in DOM ?
ANSWER
According to DOM Level 2 specification it has following main objects.

- **Attribute**: Represents an element attribute.
- **Attributes**: Represents a collection of attribute.
- **CDATASection** : Represents an XML CDATA section.
- **Comment**: Represents an XML comment.
- **Document**: Represents an XML document.
- **Element**: Represents an XML element node.
- **Node**: Represents a generic node object in an XML document.
- **NodeList**: Represents an ordered collection of node objects.
- **ProcessingInstruction**: Represents an XML processing instruction.
- **TextNode**: Represents an XML text node.

Q. What are the different properties involved in DOM ?
ANSWER
According to DOM Level 2 specification it has following main properties

- **name**: It has the name of the Attribute.
- **namespaceURI**: It represents namespace URI of the

node.

- **nextSibling**: It contains the next sibling of the Node in document source order.
- **nodeName**: This represents name of the node.
- **nodeType**: It represents type of the node.
- **nodeValue**: It has value of the node.
- **ownerDocument**: It has reference to the Document object that contains the Node.
- **ownerElement**: It has reference of the Element to which the Attribute belongs.
- **parentNode**: It represents parent Node to which the node belongs.
- **prefix**: It represents namespace prefix of the node.
- **previousSibling** : It has the previous sibling of the Node in document source order.
- **text**: It has contents of all the text nodes contained by the Node and any element nodes that it contains.
- **value**: It has value of the Attribute.
- **attributes**: Represents collection of Attribute objects.
- **childNodes**: Represents NodeList collection of node objects.
- **data**: Represents text stored within a TextNode, CDATASection, or Comment.
- **documentElement**: It contains root element node of the document.
- **firstChild**: This is first child of the Node in document source order.
- **lastChild**: This is the last child of the Node object in document source order.
- **length**: It represents number of elements in the collection.
- **localName**: It has local name of the node..

Q. What is windows load event?

ANSWER

Load event occurs generally fired after the object is completely loaded. Window load event is event occurs when images, script files, CSS files and other dependencies get loaded. Below screenshot shows use of load event.

Q. What is DOM ready event?

ANSWER

DOM ready event get fired when elements are get loaded to browser. It does not wait for images and other files loaded. We can listen to this event by attaching a callback method. A method can be added to **readyStateChange** or **DOMContentLoaded**.The below code shows the use of these events.

```
<!DOCTYPE html>
<html>
```

```
<head>
 <title>Window Ready Event Example</title>
  <script>
   var readyHandler = function(){
    var element = document.querySelector("#message1");
    element.innerHTML = "Ready Handler Fired :
readystatechange <span style='color:blue'>"+new Date()+"
</span>"
    }
   document.onreadystatechange = readyHandler;
  </script>
  <script>
  document.addEventListener("DOMContentLoaded",
function(event) {
    var element = document.querySelector("#message2");
    element.innerHTML = " Ready Handler Fired :
DOMContentLoaded <span style='color:red'>"+new
Date()+"</span>";
  });
</script>
</head>
<body>
 <h2 id="message1">
 </h2>
 <h2 id="message2">
 </h2>
</body>
</html>
```

The following screenshot shows the output of the above code.

Ready Handler Fired : readystatechange Sun Jul 20 2014 20:14:40 GMT+0530 (India Standard Time)

Ready Handler Fired : DOMContentLoaded Sun Jul 20 2014 20:14:40 GMT+0530 (India Standard Time)

```
<!DOCTYPE html>
<html>
  <head>
      <title>Window Ready Event Example</title>
    <script>
    <script>
  </head>
  <body>
    <h2 id="message1">
    <h2 id="message2">
  </body>
</html>
```

Q. What is query selector in DOM?

ANSWER

DOM provides **querySelector()** and **querySelectorAll()** methods for selecting DOM elements. querySelector() method return a single element which matches first in the DOM. querySelectorAll() method return a node list of matched elements. Below code demonstrates the use of these methods in selecting elements from DOM.

```
<!DOCTYPE html>
<html>
<head>
 <title>Document Query Selector Example</title>
</head>
<body>
 <h5 class="name">Sandeep Kumar Patel</h5>
 <h4 class="country">India</h4>
 <h4 class="country">UK</h4>
 <h5 class="name">Surabhi Patel</h5>
```

```html
    <h4 class="country">US</h4>
    <h4 id="my-score">520</h4>
    <script>
       var element = document.querySelector( "#my-score" );
       element.style.color="red";
       var elements = document.querySelectorAll("h4#my-score,
    h5.name");
       for (var item of elements) {
         item.style.fontStyle = "Italic";
       }
       var aElement = document.querySelector( "h4.country,
    h4#my-score" );
       aElement.style.background = "orange";
    </script>
</body>
</html>
```

The following screenshot shows the output of the above code in Browser.

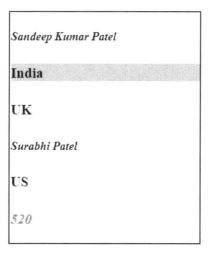

Q. What is primary Data Type of DOM?
Node interface is the primary data type of DOM. It represents a single item from DOM tree. Document, Element, CharacterData, ProcessingInstruction, DocumentFragment, DocumentType, Notation, Entity, EntityReference interface inherits from Node interface.

Q. What is document fragment in DOM?
DocumentFragment is a light weight version of DOM. It does not have any parent class. It is generally used by the developer as a temporary storage of DOM elements. Below code shows an Example of creating document fragment and adding HTML element to it and finally placing it to the body of the DOM.

```
<!DOCTYPE html>
<html>
<head>
 <title>DocumentFragment Example</title>
</head>
<body>
  <script>
   var aFragment = document.createDocumentFragment(),
      aHTMLElement = document.createElement("h2"),
      aTEXTElement = document.createTextNode("SANDEEP");
   aHTMLElement.appendChild(aTEXTElement);
   aFragment.appendChild(aHTMLElement);
   document.body.appendChild(aFragment);
  </script>
</body>
</html>
```

Below screenshot shows an h2 element with a child text node containing value SANDEEP is place inside document fragment. Finally the document fragment is appended as a child to the body element.

Q. Which is basic object of DOM?
ANSWER

Node is most basic object of DOM. It is the most common interface from which lot of other DOM object are inherited. The following interfaces all inherit from Node its methods and properties: Document, Element, CharacterData, ProcessingInstruction, DocumentFragment, DocumentType, Notation, Entity, EntityReference. These interfaces may return null in particular cases where the methods and properties are not relevant. They may throw an exception - for example when adding children to a node type for which no children can exist.

Q. What are the common doctype declarations?
ANSWER

There are 8 different type of doctype declaration and are listed below.

- **HTML 5**: This document type is used in HTML5.

  ```
  <!DOCTYPE html>
  ```

- **HTML 4.01 Strict**: This DTD contains all HTML elements and attributes, but does NOT INCLUDE presentational or deprecated elements (like font). Framesets are not allowed.

  ```
  <!DOCTYPE HTML PUBLIC "-//W3C//DTD HTML 4.01//EN" "http://www.w3.org/TR/html4/strict.dtd">
  ```

- **HTML 4.01 Transitional**: This DTD contains all HTML elements and attributes, INCLUDING presentational and deprecated elements (like font). Framesets are not allowed.

  ```
  <!DOCTYPE HTML PUBLIC "-//W3C//DTD HTML 4.01 Transitional//EN" "http://www.w3.org/TR/html4/loose.dtd">
  ```

- **HTML 4.01 Frameset**: This DTD is equal to HTML 4.01 Transitional, but allows the use of frameset content.

  ```
  <!DOCTYPE HTML PUBLIC "-//W3C//DTD HTML 4.01 Frameset//EN" "http://www.w3.org/TR/html4/frameset.dtd">
  ```

- **XHTML 1.0 Strict**: This DTD contains all HTML elements and attributes, but does NOT INCLUDE presentational or deprecated elements (like font). Framesets are not allowed. The markup must also be written as well-formed XML.

  ```
  <!DOCTYPE html PUBLIC "-//W3C//DTD XHTML 1.0 Strict//EN" "http://www.w3.org/TR/xhtml1/DTD/xhtml1-strict.dtd">
  ```

- **XHTML 1.0 Transitional**: This DTD contains all HTML elements and attributes, INCLUDING presentational and deprecated elements (like font). Framesets are not allowed. The markup must also be written as well-formed XML.

  ```
  <!DOCTYPE html PUBLIC "-//W3C//DTD XHTML 1.0
  Transitional//EN"
  "http://www.w3.org/TR/xhtml1/DTD/xhtml1-
  transitional.dtd">
  ```

- **XHTML 1.0 Frameset**: This DTD is equal to XHTML 1.0 Transitional, but allows the use of frameset content.

  ```
  <!DOCTYPE html PUBLIC "-//W3C//DTD XHTML 1.0
  Frameset//EN"
  "http://www.w3.org/TR/xhtml1/DTD/xhtml1-
  frameset.dtd">
  ```

- **XHTML 1.1**: This DTD is equal to XHTML 1.0 Strict, but allows you to add modules (for example to provide ruby support for East-Asian languages).

  ```
  <!DOCTYPE html PUBLIC "-//W3C//DTD XHTML
  1.1//EN"
  "http://www.w3.org/TR/xhtml11/DTD/xhtml11.dtd"
  >
  ```

Chapter 6 Date Object

Q. What is a JavaScript Date Object?

ANSWER

JavaScript Date object returns time in that single moment. It contains the value in number of milliseconds since 1 January, 1970 UTC.

Q. What are the different ways to create a Date object? Or what are the different constructor forms of Date object?

ANSWER

JavaScript Date object has 4 overloaded constructors. These constructors are listed below.

> new Date()
> new Date(milliseconds)
> new Date(dateString)
> new Date(year, month, day, hours, minutes, seconds, milliseconds)

Q. How to get 1st January 1970 in a date object, the date from where time is gets calculated?

ANSWER

1st January 1970 is the day from where the time is get calculated as number of milliseconds elapsed. It can be calculated by creating a new JS object with parameter 0.below screenshot demonstrate the date object with parameter 0.

Q. How JavaScript counts months?

ANSWER

JavaScript counts months from 0 to 11 for the twelve months a year. 0 represents January and 11 represent December. Below screenshot shows the code for today's date that is July 23 and year 2014 and **getMonth()** returns 6.

Q. When RangeError invalid date exception occurs?

ANSWER

When a date object is created with invalid date string and **toISOString()** method is applied to this invalid date then this RangeError occurs. Below screenshot shows '2014-13-13' string which is representing YYYY-MM-DD format where month is out of range produces the RangeError exception.

```
> var date = new
  Date('2014-13-13');
  console.log(date.toISOString());
```

RangeError: invalid date
```
  var date = new Date('2014-13-13');

  console.log(date.toISOString());
```

```
1  var date = new Date('2014-13-13');
2
3  console.log(date.toISOString());
```

Chapter 7 Regular Expression

Regular expressions are used for pattern matching in a string. A regular expression in JavaScript can be declared in two ways. Syntax for these two approaches is listed below.

```
var aRegExpression = new RegExp(pattern,modifiers);
var aRegExpression = /pattern/modifiers;
```

The details of these syntaxes are as follows:
- **pattern** : it represents the search string.
- **modifiers** : it represents the conditional switches that will be applied to the pattern matching

There are 3 different methods for regular expressions are listed below.
- **exec()** : scans for a matching string and returns the first matched string
- **test()** : scans for a matching string and returns boolean value false or true.
- **toString()** : This method returns the string value of a regular expression.

The \w represents an alphanumeric character. The following code demonstrate the use of \w switch .

```
var regEx= /\wu/;
```

```
var out1 = regEx.exec("sandeep Ku Patel"),
    out2 = regEx.test("sandeep Ku Patel");
console.log(out1);
console.log(out2);
```

Below screenshot shows the output of the above code which pattern match any substring having alphanumeric character with 2nd character as u.

⚑ ⚑ ‹ › ⟫ **Console ▾** HTML CSS Script DOM Net Cookies Page Speed Typography	

⟲ Clear Persist Profile | Run Clear Copy Pretty Print History	

```
var regEx= /\wu/;  var   1  var regEx= /\wu/;
out1 =                     2
regEx.exec("sandeep...     3  var out1 = regEx.exec("sandeep Ku Patel"),
Patel");                   4      out2 = regEx.test("sandeep Ku Patel");
                           5
console.log(out1);         6  console.log(out1);
console.log(out2);         7  console.log(out2);|

  ⊕ [ "Ku" ]

  true
```

Q. Write a Regular expression to reverse the first and last name? For example Sandeep Patel becomes Patel Sandeep.
ANSWER
To reverse first and last name we have to use **replace()** function on input string with regular expression. The following code shows the method to reverse first and last name.

```
var reverseFirstLastName = function(nameString){
  var regex = /(\w+)\s(\w+)/,
     resultString = nameString.replace(regex, '$2 $1');
  return resultString;
};

var inputName = "Sandeep Patel",
   output = reverseFirstLastName(inputName);
console.log(output);
```

The following screenshot shows the chrome console executing above code and output is printed on console.

```
Q    Elements  Network  Sources  Timeline  Profiles  Resources  Audits  Console
    Y   <top frame>              ▼  Preserve log
> var reverseFirstLastName = function(nameString){
    var regex = /(\w+)\s(\w+)/,
        resultString = nameString.replace(regex, '$2 $1');
    return resultString;
  };

  var inputName = "Sandeep Patel",
      output = reverseFirstLastName(inputName);
  console.log(output);
  Patel Sandeep
```

Q. Write a Regular expression to validate email address?
ANSWER
To validate email we have to use **test()** method on input string which returns true or false on execution. The following code shows the method to validate email string.

```
function validateEmail(email) {
    var re =
/^((([^<>()[\]\\.,;:\s@\"]+(\.[^<>()[\]\\.,;:\s@\"]+)*)|(\".+\"))@((\
[[0-9]{1,3}\.[0-9]{1,3}\.[0-9]{1,3}\.[0-9]{1,3}\])|(([a-zA-Z\-0-
9]+\.)+[a-zA-Z]{2,}))$/;
    return re.test(email);
};

var email1 = "sandeeppateltech@gmail.com",
    email2 = "sandeep@@gmail.com",
    result1 = validateEmail(email1),
    result2 = validateEmail(email2);

console.log(result1);
console.log(result2);
```

The following screenshot shows the output of the email validation code in a chrome developer console.

```
Q  🔲  Elements  Network  Sources  Timeline  »  ≥≡  ✿  ▭,  ×
🚫  ▽  <top frame>                ▼  ☐ Preserve log
> function validateEmail(email) {
      var re = /^(([^<>()[\]\\.,;:\s@\"]+(\.[^<>()
  [\]\\.,;:\s@\"]+)*)|(\".+\"))@((\[[0-9]{1,3}\.[0-9]
  {1,3}\.[0-9]{1,3}\.[0-9]{1,3}\])|(([a-zA-Z\-0-9]+\.)+
  [a-zA-Z]{2,}))$/;
      return re.test(email);
  };

  var email1 = "sandeeppateltech@gmail.com",
      email2 = "sandeep@@gmail.com",
      result1 = validateEmail(email1),
      result2 = validateEmail(email2);

  console.log(result1);
  console.log(result2);

  true                                           VM444:12
  false                                          VM444:13
```

Q. Write a Regular expression to validate a URL ?
ANSWER
For validating URL we have considered the protocol will be either
http/https/ftp and it must start with **WWW** word .Considering
these points the javascript code for validating a URL is as follows.

```
function validateURL(url) {
    var regExUrl = new RegExp("(http|ftp|https)://[\w-]+(\.[\w-
]+)+([\w.,@?^=%&amp;:/~+#-]*[\w@?^=%&amp;/~+#-])?");
    return regExUrl.test(url);
};
var url1 = "http://www.google.com",
    url2 = "htttp://www.google.com",
    result1 = validateURL(url1),
    result2 = validateURL(url2);

console.log(result1);
```

```
        console.log(result2);
```

The following screenshot shows the chrome console with URL validation code in execution for a given URL.

```
Q  📋   Elements  Network  Sources  Timeline  »    >≡  ⚙  🖵,  ×

🚫  🍷    <top frame>              ▼  ☐ Preserve log
> function validateURL(url) {
      var regExUrl = new RegExp("
  (http|ftp|https)://[\w-]+(\.[\w-]+)+([\w.,@?
  ^=%&amp;:/~+#-]*[\w@?^=%&amp;/~+#-])?");
      return regExUrl.test(url);
  };
  var url1 = "http://www.google.com",
      url2 = "htttp://www.google.com",
      result1 = validateURL(url1),
      result2 = validateURL(url2);

  console.log(result1);
  console.log(result2);

  true                                       VM112:11
  false                                      VM112:12
```

Chapter 8 Questions on Canvas API

Q. What is a canvas in HTML5?
ANSWER
Canvas is a new element in HTML5 for drawing graphics. A graphics can be drawn on canvas by following below steps.

- Define the canvas area.
- Get the drawing context.
- Using the context start the drawing.

Q. What is the difference between Canvas and SVG?
ANSWER
Difference between Canvas and SVG (Scalable Vector Graphics) are listed in below table.

CANVAS	SVG
i. A diagram can be drawn using a context in Canvas.	i. A diagram is drawn using XML like SVG element.
ii. A diagram drawn in canvas is resolution dependent.	ii. A diagram drawn in SVG is resolution independent.
iii. A diagram drawn in Canvas can be saved to PNG or JPG format.	iii. SVG diagrams cannot be saved to PNG or JPG format.
iv. Diagram drawn in Canvas is pixel based. No DOM elements are involved.	iv. Diagram drawn in SVG is DOM element based. No pixels are involved in the diagram.
v. Rendering game graphics, such as sprites and backgrounds can be created.	v. Highly interactive animated user interfaces can be created.

vi.	Poor text rendering capabilities		vi.	Good text rendering capabilities
vii.	Poor SEO and Accessibility as everything pixel based and content are not accessible.		vii.	Better SEO and Accessibility as it DOM based rendering.
viii.	Modified through script only.		viii.	Modified through script and CSS.
ix.	Performance is better with smaller surface, a larger number of objects (>10k), or both.		ix.	Performance is better with smaller number of objects (<10k), a larger surface, or both.

Q. What is canvas 2d context and how it is created?

ANSWER'

Using **getContext()** method with parameter **'2d'** a canvas context can be created.

This context method is a type of **CanvasRenderingContext2D** object. Below code shows a simple 2d context creation and log the object's constructor.

```html
<html>
 <body>
 <canvas id="myCanvas"></canvas>
 <script>
  var canvas = document.getElementById("myCanvas"),
  context = canvas.getContext("2d");
  console.log(context.constructor);
 </script>
 </body>
</html>
```

The following screenshot shows the constructor function of the context object which is CanvasRenderingContext2D native object.

Q. How to load an image in Canvas?

ANSWER

An image can be loaded using **drawImage()** method. This method takes several inputs for drawing an image. These parameters are positioning and clipping type. We will discuss these parameters in separate question. Below code shows how to use the **drawImage()** method to load a PNG image from a URL inside the canvas.

```
<html>
<body>
  <canvas id="myCanvas"></canvas>
  <script>
    var canvas = document.getElementById("myCanvas"),
      context = canvas.getContext("2d"),
      img = new Image();
    img.src =
"http://www.gravatar.com/avatar/4205261332ff131e971b48db
31dcb528.png";
    img.onload = function() {
      context.drawImage(img, 10, 10);
    };
  </script>
</body>
```

</html>

Below screenshot shows the Gravatar image getting drawn inside the HTML5 canvas element. This drawing is done using 2d context.

Q. what are the different overloaded signature for drawImage() method?

ANSWER

The **drawImage()** method has 3 different signature and listed below.

- **drawImage(img, x, y)** :This method position the image on the canvas at **<x, y>** coordinates.

- **drawImage(img, x, y, width, height)** : This method position the image on the canvas at **<x, y>** coordinates with a specified **height**.

- **drawImage(img, sx, sy, swidth, sheight, x, y, width, height)** : This method clipped the image with starting point **<sx, sy>** having height **sheight** and width **swidth** and position it at **<x, y>** coordinates with a specified **height** and **width**.

Chapter 9 Geo Location API

Q. What is Geo Location API?
ANSWER
Geo Location API publishes the location of the user to the web. It needs user's permission for privacy reason. The Geo location API is present inside **navigator.geolocation** object.

Q. How to determine Geo Location API is supported in browser?
ANSWER
To determine Geo location API is supported in browser can be determined by the truth value of geolocation object inside the navigator object. Below code has the function which returns true or false Boolean value based on the geolocation object present inside the navigator.

```
function isGeoLocationSupported(){
  var flag = navigator.geolocation ? true : false;
  return flag;
}
var isSupported = isGeoLocationSupported();
if(isSupported){
  console.log(navigator.geolocation);
}else{
  console.log("Geo Location API not supprted");
}
```

The following screenshot shows the output of the above code as the geolocation object is present inside the navigator API.

```
function                              1  function isGeoLocationSupported(){
 isGeoLocationSupported(){            2     var flag = navigator.geolocation ? true : false;
 var flag ...nsole.log("Geo          3     return flag;
 Location API not                    4  }
 supprted");     )                   5  var isSupported = isGeoLocationSupported();
Geolocation {                        6  if(isSupported){
getCurrentPosition=getCurrentPosition(),   7     console.log(navigator.geolocation);
watchPosition=watchPosition(),       8  }else{
clearWatch=clearWatch() }            9     console.log("Geo Location API not supprted");
                                    10  }
```

Chapter 10 Web Workers

Q. What is a Web Worker?
ANSWER

Q. What is a Web Worker?
ANSWER
Web Workers are new HTML5 feature to achieve concurrency in JavaScript execution in web application. A web worker is JavaScript file which run in the background of the browser without impacting the page performance. This helps in resolve the age old problem "**Un responsive script alert box**". Generally these workers can be used for extensive computation purpose.

Q. How to detect Web Worker is supported by browser?
ANSWER
We can check the support of Web Worker in a browser by validating the Worker property is present in the window object. Code for checking Web Worker support is as follows:

```html
<!DOCTYPE html>
<html>
<head lang="en">
  <title>Web Worker</title>
</head>
<body>
  <script>
    var isWorkerSupported = window.Worker ? true : false;
    console.log("Is Web Worker Supported: "+isWorkerSupported);
  </script>
</body>
</html>
```

In the previous code isWorkerSupported variable can contain TRUE or FALSE value based on the existence of Worker property inside window object. The following screenshot shows the output of above code in chrome console.

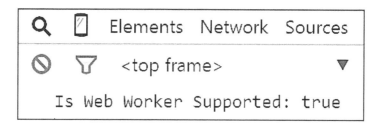

Q. What is a dedicated worker?
ANSWER
A dedicated worker is only accessible by the calling script. A dedicated worker object can be created using worker constructor. Syntax for creating a new dedicated worker is listed below.

```
var aDedicatedWorker = new Worker("script.js")
```

The parameter inside the Worker object is the JavaScript file which will run as worker in the background of the browser.

Q. What is a shared worker?
ANSWER
A Shared Worker can be accessed by multiple scripts. A shared worker is accessible by different window, iframe and by other worker having same origin. Syntax for creating a new dedicated worker is as follows.

```
var aSharedWorker = new SharedWorker("script.js")
```

The parameter inside the Worker object is the JavaScript file which will run as shared worker in the background of the browser.

Q. Develop a dedicated worker to display the time?
ANSWER

Let's create the time worker in **dateWorker.js** file and we can call this worker in **dateWorkerDemo.html** file. The following code shows the content of **dateWorker.js** file which listens to the messages and posts the current time in every second.

```
self.addEventListener("message",function(event){
    setInterval(function(){
        var time = new Date();
        self.postMessage({
            hour:time.getHours(),
            minute: time.getMinutes(),
            second: time.getSeconds()
        });
    },1000);
});
```

The following code shows the content of **dateWorkerDemo.html** containing creation of worker instance and listening to worker response.

```
<!DOCTYPE html>
<html>
<head lang="en">
    <meta charset="UTF-8">
    <title>Time Web Worker Demo</title>
</head>
<body>
<h1 id="resultContainer"></h1>
<button id="timeButton">Get Time</button>

<script>
    var dateWorker = new Worker("dateWorker.js"),
        resultContainer = document.getElementById("resultContainer"),
        timeButton = document.getElementById("timeButton");

    timeButton.addEventListener("click",function(){
        dateWorker.postMessage(null);
    });
    dateWorker.addEventListener("message",function(workerEvent){
        var responseData = workerEvent.data,
            hour = responseData.hour,
            minute = responseData.minute,
            second = responseData.second;
        resultContainer.innerText = "HOUR: "+hour +
```

```
    " MINUTE: "+minute +" SECOND: "+second;
  });
</script>
</body>
</html>
```

The output of the preceding code shown in following screenshot with hour, minute and second is displayed from the worker response messages.

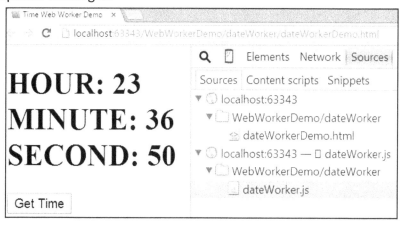

Q. Develop a dedicated worker to find square of a number?
ANSWER
The definition of square worker is present in **doSquareWorker.js** file and listens to message and generates the square of number. The square worker is instantiated in **squareWorkerDemo.html** file which listens to the response from the square worker and prints it in browser.The code content of **doSquareWorker.js** file are as follows.

```
self.addEventListener("message",function(event){
  var inputData = event.data,
    inputNumber = parseInt(inputData.number,10),
    squareResult = Math.pow(inputNumber,2);
  self.postMessage({result:squareResult});
});
```

The **squareWorkerDemo**.html file has the following code.

```html
<!DOCTYPE html>
<html>
<head lang="en">
  <meta charset="UTF-8">
  <title>Square Web Worker Demo</title>
</head>
<body>

  <h1 id="resultContainer"></h1>
  <input type="number" id="inputNumber" placeholder="Enter a number" value="5">
  <button id="squareButton"> SQUARE</button>

  <script>
    var squareWorker = new Worker("doSquareWorker.js"),
        resultContainer = document.getElementById("resultContainer"),
        squareButton = document.getElementById("squareButton"),
        inputNumber=document.getElementById("inputNumber");

    squareButton.addEventListener("click",function(){
      squareWorker.postMessage({number:inputNumber.value});
    });

    squareWorker.addEventListener("message",function(workerEvent){
      var responseData = workerEvent.data,
          squareResult= responseData.result;
      resultContainer.innerText = squareResult;
    });
  </script>
</body>
</html>
```

The output of the preceding code shown in following screenshot
with square of a number is displayed from the worker response
messages.

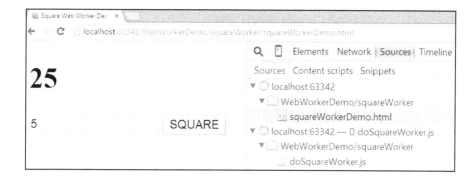

Q. How to define an inline web worker? Demonstrate an inline worker for multiplying 2 numbers?

ANSWER

An inline web worker can be defined inside a HTML markup using **<script>** tag with **type** attribute having value **javascript/worker**.
Syntax:

```
<script type="javascript/worker">
//JavaScript Code for defining a worker
</script>
```

Example:

The **inlineWorkerDemo.html** file contains the code for defining multiplication worker which listens to the messages and calculates the multiplication and post the response. The listener to the multiply worker extracts the result and renders in the browser. The following code shows the content of **inlineWorkerDemo.html** file.

```
<!DOCTYPE html>
<html>
<head lang="en">
  <meta charset="UTF-8">
  <title>Inline Web Worker Demo</title>
</head>
<body>
<h1 id="resultContainer"></h1>
<input type="number" id="number1" value="8" placeholder="Enter first number">
<input type="number" id="number2" value="10" placeholder="Enter second number">
```

```html
<button id="multiplyButton">Multiply</button>
<script id="multiplyWorker" type="javascript/worker">
  self.addEventListener("message",function(event){
    var requestData = event.data,
      number1 = requestData.number1,
      number2 = requestData.number2,
      multiplyResult = number1 * number2;
    self.postMessage({result:multiplyResult});
  });
</script>
<script>
  var textContent = document.querySelector('#multiplyWorker').textContent,
    workerBlob = new Blob([textContent]),
    workerURL = window.URL.createObjectURL(workerBlob),
    multiplyWorker = new Worker(workerURL),
    resultContainer = document.getElementById("resultContainer"),
    multiplyButton = document.getElementById("multiplyButton"),
    number1 = document.getElementById("number1"),
    number2 = document.getElementById("number2");
  multiplyButton.addEventListener("click", function () {
    multiplyWorker.postMessage({
      number1:parseInt(number1.value,10),
      number2: parseInt(number2.value,10)
    });
  });
  multiplyWorker.addEventListener("message", function (workerEvent) {
    var responseData = workerEvent.data,
        result = responseData.result;
    resultContainer.innerText = "Result: " + result;
  });
</script>
</body>
</html>
```

User can input two numbers in the text box and press the multiply button. The multiply worker calculate the multiplication and result is rendered in the browser. The outputs of the preceding code are rendered as following screenshot.

Q. How to handle error in web worker?

ANSWER

We can throw error using **throw** keyword from the web worker. A callback method can be attached to the **error** event to handle the generated error. The **positiveNoSqaureWorkerDemo.html** file contains a worker which takes only positive number as input. If a negative number is passed it throws an error. The code content of this file is as follows.

```
<!DOCTYPE html>
<html>
<head lang="en">
  <meta charset="UTF-8">
  <title>Web Worker Error Handler Demo</title>
</head>
<body>
<h1 id="resultContainer"></h1>
<input type="number" id="number1" value="-4" placeholder="Enter a number">
<button id="squareResult">Square</button>
<script id="squareWorker" type="javascript/worker">
  self.addEventListener("message",function(event){
    var requestData = event.data,
      number1 = requestData.number1,
      squareResult = 0;
    if(number1>0) {
      squareResult = number1 * number1
      self.postMessage({result:squareResult});
    } else{
```

```
            //For negative number throw error
            throw "It is a negative number.Please supply a positive number.";
        }
    });
</script>
<script>
    var textContent = document.querySelector('#squareWorker').textContent,
        workerBlob = new Blob([textContent]),
        workerURL = window.URL.createObjectURL(workerBlob),
        squareWorker = new Worker(workerURL),
        resultContainer = document.getElementById("resultContainer"),
        squareResult = document.getElementById("squareResult"),
        number1 = document.getElementById("number1"),
        number2 = document.getElementById("number2");
    squareResult.addEventListener("click", function () {
        squareWorker.postMessage({
            number1:parseInt(number1.value,10)
        });
    });
    //Success Handler for the worker
    squareWorker.addEventListener("message", function (workerEvent) {
        var responseData = workerEvent.data,
            result = responseData.result;
        resultContainer.innerText = "Result: " + result;
    });
    //Error Handler for the worker
    squareWorker.addEventListener('error', function(workerErrorEvent){
        resultContainer.innerText = "Error: " + workerErrorEvent.message;
    }, false);
</script>
</body>
</html>
```

The output of the above code is rendered as following screenshot
rendering the error message in the browser.

Q. How to import an external script in web worker? Demonstrate it with an example?

ANSWER

To import external script inside a web worker we need to use **importScripts()** method with a file name as input parameter. To demonstrate import script functionality we have created 3 files **greatest-number-script.js, numberWorker.js, numberWorkerDemo.html** file. The following screenshot shows these files.

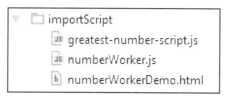

The **greatest-number-script.js** is the external script that we need to import it to our web worker. It has a single method **findGreatestNumber()** method to find out a bigger number among two supplied numbers. The following code shows the content of **greatest-number-script.js** file.

```
var findGreatestNumber = function(number1,number2){
    return number1>number2 ? number1 : number2;
};
```

The **numberWorker.js** file contains the code for importing the external script inside the web worker message listener callback method. The following code shows the content of **numberWorker.js** file.

```
self.addEventListener("message",function(event){
    var numberWorker = self.importScripts('greatest-number-script.js');
    var requestData = event.data,
        number1 = requestData.number1,
        number2 = requestData.number2,
```

```
    greatestNumber = findGreatestNumber(number1,number2);
    self.postMessage({result:greatestNumber});
  });
```

The **numberWorkerDemo.html** file contains the code for instantiating the number web worker and listening to response message. The following code shows the content of **numberWorkerDemo.html** file.

```
<!DOCTYPE html>
<html>
<head lang="en">
  <meta charset="UTF-8">
  <title>Time Web Worker Demo</title>
</head>
<body>
<h1 id="resultContainer"></h1>
<input type="number" id="number1" value="7" placeholder="Enter first number">
<input type="number" id="number2" value="9" placeholder="Enter second
number">
<button id="greatButton">Find Greatest Number</button>
<script>
  var numberWorker = new Worker("numberWorker.js"),
    resultContainer = document.getElementById("resultContainer"),
    greatButton = document.getElementById("greatButton"),
    number1 = document.getElementById("number1"),
    number2=document.getElementById("number2");
  greatButton.addEventListener("click",function(){
    numberWorker.postMessage({
      number1:parseInt(number1.value,10),
      number2: parseInt(number2.value,10)
    });
  });
  numberWorker.addEventListener("message",function(workerEvent){
    var responseData = workerEvent.data;
    resultContainer.innerText = "Greatest Number: "+responseData.result;
  });
</script>
</body>
</html>
```

The output of this code is rendered as following screenshot containing the greatest number from the supplied numbers.

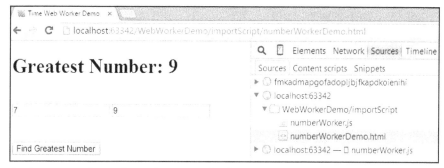

Q. Create a shared worker to calculate the length of a string?
ANSWER

The **calculateLengthWorker.js** contains the code for listening messages and calculates the length of input string. The shared worker listens to message in a port by listening to connect event. The code for **calculateLengthWorker.js** file is as follows.

```
self.addEventListener("connect", function (event) {
  var port = event.ports[0];
  port.addEventListener("message", function (event) {
    var requestData = event.data,
      inputString = requestData.string,
      stringLength = inputString.length;
    port.postMessage({result:stringLength});
  }, false);
  port.start();
}, false);
```

The **lengthWorkerDemo.html** file contains the code for instantiating the shared worker and rendering the response in browser. The code content of **lengthWorkerDemo.html** file are listed as follows.

```
<!DOCTYPE html>
<html>
<head lang="en">
  <meta charset="UTF-8">
  <title>Shared Web Worker Demo</title>
</head>
<body>
```

```
<h1 id="resultContainer"></h1>
<input type="text" id="inputString" value="Hello" placeholder="Enter a string">
<button id="lengthButton">Get Length</button>
<script>
    var lengthWorker = new SharedWorker("calculateLengthWorker.js"),
        resultContainer = document.getElementById("resultContainer"),
        lengthButton = document.getElementById("lengthButton"),
        inputString = document.getElementById("inputString");

    lengthButton.addEventListener("click", function () {
        resultContainer.innerText = "";
        lengthWorker.port.postMessage({
            string:inputString.value
        });
    });
    //start the worker
    lengthWorker.port.start();
    //Success Handler for the worker
    lengthWorker.port.addEventListener("message", function (workerEvent) {
        var responseData = workerEvent.data,
            result = responseData.result;
        resultContainer.innerText = "Result: " + result;
    });
</script>
</body>
</html>
```

The output of the preceding code is rendered as following
screenshot displaying length of the input string.

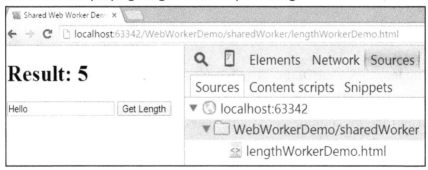

Chapter 11 Local Storage

HTML5 provides a feature to store data locally in end user's browser. Data is stored in the browser as key-value pair. Unlike cookie it has average space of 5 MB. This storage comes in 2 different type sessionStorage and localStorage.

- **localStorage** : it stores data with no expiration date.
- **sessionStorage** : it stores data with an expiration date.

window.Storage() is the main interface from where the localStorage and sessionStorage are implemented. This interface has the below definition.

```
interface Storage {
  readonly attribute unsigned long length;
  DOMString? key(unsigned long index);
  getter DOMString? getItem(DOMString key);
  setter creator void setItem(DOMString key, DOMString value);
  deleter void removeItem(DOMString key);
  void clear();
}
```

The details of the above code are as follows:-

- **setItem(key,value)** : This methods stored the value in storage using **key-value** pair.
- **getItem(key)** : This method retrieves the stored object using the key.
- **removeItem(key)** : This methods removes the stored item based on the key.
- **clear()** : Deletes all the items from the storage.

- **length** : This property returns the length of the storage, no of elements inside the storage.
- **key(position)** : This method returns the key for the value in the given numeric position.

Q. How to store and retrieve an object in local storage?
ANSWER
Local storage provides setItem() and getItem() for storing and retrieving an object from the storage. **setItem(key, value)** method takes 2 input parameter to store the object. The **getItem(key)** method retrieves the value using key as input parameter. Below code shows the storing **"Sandeep Kumar"** string in **"myName"** key and then retrieves this string place it in a HTML element.

```
<!DOCTYPE html>
<html>
 <body>
  <div id="resultContainer">
  </div>
   <script>
    var container =
document.getElementById("resultContainer");
     localStorage.setItem("myName", "Sandeep Kumar");
     container.innerHTML = localStorage.getItem("myName");
   </script>
 </body>
</html>
```

Below screenshot shows the chrome developer storage preview which holds the above object as key and value pair.

Sandeep Kumar

| Q | Elements | Network | Sources | Timeline | Profiles |

		Key	Value
▶ ☐ Frames		myName	Sandeep Kumar
🗄 Web SQL			
🗄 IndexedDB			
▼ ⊞ Local Storage			
⊞ http://127.0.0.1:51792			
▶ ⊞ Session Storage			
▶ 🍪 Cookies			
⊞ Application Cache			

Q. How to attach an event to a local storage?
ANSWER
When local storage objects get modified a storage event is fired. A callback method can be attached to window object using **addEventListener()** or **attachEvent()** method.

NOTE:
When the **setItem(), removeItem(),** and **clear()** methods are called on a Storage object x that is associated with a local storage area, if the methods did something, then in every Document object whose Window object's localStorage attribute's Storage object is associated with the same storage area, other than x, a storage event must be fired.

In simple sentence, a storage event is fired on every window/tab except for the one that updated the localStorage object and caused the event. Below code has a callback method listening to storage event. When the button is clicked in one of the tab to update the local storage object the storage event listener in the other tab got triggered and content is updated.

```
<!DOCTYPE html>
```

```html
<html>
 <body>
  <div id="resultContainer"> </div>
  <button onclick="update()">Click Me</button>
  <script>
   var container =
document.getElementById("resultContainer"),
     methodStorageEvent = function(event){
     container.innerHTML = "Event
Fired"+localStorage.getItem("myName") ;
     },
     counter = 1,
     update = function(){
       localStorage.setItem("myName", ++counter);
       container.innerHTML =
localStorage.getItem("myName") ;
     };
     window.addEventListener("storage",
methodStorageEvent,false)
   </script>
 </body>
</html>
```

Below screenshot demonstrates how the storage event is fired and the other tabs which accessing the same page receives the storage event and update their content.

Chapter 12 File API

HTML5 provides new API to work with files inside a browser. This API provides File, FileList and Blob data type to work with files. It provide FileReader interface to read files asynchronously.

FileReader provides 4 different methods to work with loaded files. These asynchronous methods are listed as follows.

- **readAsBinaryString(Blob | File)** : Reads the target file and save it to binary string containing integer of range 0-255.

- **readAsText(Blob | File, opt_encoding)**: Reads the target file and save it as UTF-8 text file.

- **readAsDataURL(Blob | File)** : Reads the target file and returns a data URL containing base64 ascii string.

- **readAsArrayBuffer(Blob | File)** : Reads the target file and save it in a array buffer.

A blob object refers to a sequence of bytes representing data. The IDL(Interface Definition Syntax) for Blob object is as follows:

```
interface Blob {
    readonly attribute unsigned long long size;
    readonly attribute DOMString type;
    Blob slice(optional [Clamp] long long start,
        optional [Clamp] long long end,
        optional DOMString contentType);
    void close();
```

```
};
```

The details of the method and properties are as follows:

- **slice method** : The slice method returns a new Blob object with bytes ranging from the optional start parameter up to but not including the optional end parameter, and with a type attribute that is the value of the optional contentType parameter

- **close method**: The close method must permanently neuter the original Blob object. This is an irreversible and non-idempotent operation; once a Blob has been neutered, it cannot be used again; dereferencing a Blob URL bound to a Blob object on which close has been called results in a network error. A neutered Blob must have a size of 0.

- **size property**: It returns the size of the Blob object in bytes.

- **type property**: It returns the type of the content that the Blob object holds.

Q. How to create a Blob Object?
ANSWER
A blob object can be created using new keyword with Blob constructor. A Blob constructor takes the following parameters:

- **Blob part sequence**: This can be either ArrayBuffer, ArrayBufferView, Blob and DOMString

- **Blob property bag**: It takes one parameter representing type of the ASCII-encoded string in lower case representing the media type of the Blob.

The following code shows an example of creating Blob using new keyword:

```
var a = new Blob();
var b = new Blob(["foobarbazetcetc" + "birdiebirdieboo"], {type:
```

"text/plain;charset=UTF-8"});

Q. What are readable states for a Blob object?
ANSWER
A Blob must have a readability state, which is one of OPENED or
CLOSED.

- A Blob that refers to a byte sequence, including one of 0
  bytes, is said to be in the OPENED readability state.

- A Blob is said to be closed if its close method has been
  called. A Blob that is closed is said to be in the CLOSED
  readability state.

Q. What are different states of FileReader?
ANSWER
The FileReader object can be in one of 3 states. The readyState
attribute, on getting, must return the current state, which must be
one of the following values:

- **EMPTY**: The FileReader object has been constructed, and
  there are no pending reads. None of the read methods have
  been called. This is the default state of a newly minted
  FileReader object, until one of the read methods have been
  called on it.

- **LOADING**: A File or Blob is being read. One of the read
  methods is being processed, and no error has occurred
  during the read.

- **DONE**: The entire File or Blob has been read into memory,
  OR a file error occurred during read, OR the read was
  aborted using abort(). The FileReader is no longer reading a
  File or Blob. If readyState is set to DONE it means at least
  one of the read methods have been called on this
  FileReader.

Chapter 13 Web RTC

Q. What is Web RTC?

ANSWER

Web RTC provides the capability to browsers for real time communication without any additional plugin installed. It involves audio, video and other type of data streaming among the browser with their native capability.

Q. What is the API implemented by Web RTC?

ANSWER

Web RTC implements three different API. These interfaces are listed below.

- **MediaStream** : This represents a synchronized media stream using camera and microphone.

- **RTCPeerConnection** : This interface is responsible for stable connection between peer browser during real time communication.

- **RTCDataChannel** : This interface is responsible for other type of data communication between peer browser. For example the remote desktop sharing using browser.

Q. What is MediaStream?

ANSWER

MediaStream basically represents the stream captured by Camera and microphone. Each MediaStream has an input which captures the stream. This MediaStream can be accessed using **navigator.getUserMedia()** method.

Q. What are the input parameters to getUserMedia() method?

ANSWER

The **getUserMedia()** method takes 3 parameters as input. These parameters are as follows:

- Constraint Object similar to a configuration object.
- Success Callback Method.
- Error Callback Method.

Q. What are MediaStreamTracks?

ANSWER

The MediaStream returned by **getUserMedia()** has 2 useful methods **getAudioTracks()** and **getVideoTracks()**.Both of these methods returns an array of **MediaStramTracks**.

Q. What are the protocols used by Web RTC for communication?

ANSWER

Web RTC uses 2 different protocols for communication. These 2 protocols are listed as follows.

- **DTLS**: Datagram Transport Layer Security.
- **SRTP**: Secure Real-time Transport Protocol.

Q. How to view the statistics of an in progress Web RTC session in Chrome browser?

ANSWER

We can view the detail statistics and charts of an ongoing Web RTC session in chrome browser by using **chrome://webrtc-internals/** in chrome browser.

Q. What are the different event handlers for a channel?

ANSWER

A channel has 4 different event handlers. These event handlers are as follows.

- **Onopen**: Executed when the connection is established.
- **Onerror**: Executed if there is an error creating the connection.

- **Onmessage**: When you receive a message, this method will execute
- **Oclose**: Executed if the other peer closes the connection.

Q. What is a signal channel?

ANSWER

WebRTC can't create connections without some sort of server in the middle. We call this the Signal Channel.

Q. What is an ICE technique?

ANSWER

Interactive Connectivity Establishment (ICE) is a technique used in computer networking involving network address translators (NATs) in Internet applications of Voice over Internet Protocol (VoIP), peer-to-peer communications, video, instant messaging and other interactive media.

Q. What is an ICE Candidate?

ANSWER

While communication peers must exchange information about the network connection. This is known as an ICE candidate.

Q. What are the server side functionalities needed by the Web RTC?

ANSWER

Web RTC requires following functionalities from server side to create a communication between peers.
- User discovery and communication.
- Signaling.
- NAT/firewall traversal.
- Relay servers in case peer-to-peer communication fails.

Q. What is STUN protocol?

ANSWER

STUN (Session Traversal Utilities for NAT) is a standardized set of methods and a network protocol to allow an end host to discover its public IP address if it is located behind a NAT.

Chapter 14 Drag & Drop API

Q. How to make content draggable inside the browser?
ANSWER
HTML5 provides drag and drop feature. An element can be made draggable by setting its draggable property to true. Check the below code having 2 buttons. One button is draggable and other is just a normal button.

```
<!DOCTYPE html>
<html>
<head>
  <title>Draggable Element</title>
</head>
<body>
  <button draggable="true">Draggable Button</button>
  <button>Normal Button</button>
</body>
</html>
```

Below screenshot shows both these buttons. The draggable button is movable while the normal button is fixed in its position.

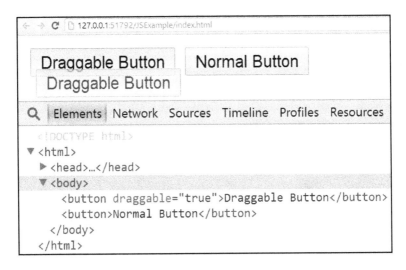

Q. What happens when drag starts for an element?
There are 3 important key points to note when a drag starts. These key points are as follows.

- **Drag Data**: It represent the type of data that will be transferred while dragging

- **Drag Feedback**: This represents image which appears beside the mouse pointer during the drag operation.

- **Drag Effect**: This represents the type of drag happens to element. It can be 3 types and listed below.

  o **Copy**: This effect indicates that the data being dragged will be copied from its present location to the drop location.

  o **Move**: This effect indicates that the data being dragged will be moved from its original position to drop location.

  o **Link**: This effect indicates that some form of relationship or connection will be created between the source and drop locations.

Q. What are the Drag and drop events?
There are 7 different drag and drop events that can be attached with a callback method programmatically.

- **Dragstart**: it is fired on an element when a drag is started
- **Dragenter**: it is fired when the mouse enters an element while a drag is occurring.
- **Dragover**: This event is fired as the mouse is moving over an

element when a drag is occurring.
- **Dragleave**: This event is fired when the mouse leaves an element while a drag is occurring.
- **Drop**: The drop event is fired on the element where the drop occurred at the end of the drag operation.
- **Dragend**: The source of the drag will receive a dragend event when the drag operation is complete, whether it was successful or not.

Q. What is a dataTransfer property?
ANSWER
dataTransfer object holds the piece of data sent in a drag action. **dataTransfer** is set in the **dragstart** event and read/handled in the drop event. The syntax for setting value in dataTransfer object is as follows.

```
event.dataTransfer.setData(format, data)
```

The above syntax will set the object's content to the mime type and data payload passed as arguments.

Q. Develop an example to drag and drop an element from one place to another?
ANSWER
To demonstrate drag and drop we have created div element with rounded border and background color red. We will drag this element and drop it in a container. The following code shows the drag and drop example.

```
<!DOCTYPE HTML>
<html>
<head>
  <style>
    #ball{
       width:50px;
       height:50px;
       background: red;
       border-radius: 100%;
```

```
      }
      #dropZone {
        width:200px;
        height:100px;
        padding:10px;
        border:1px solid #aaaaaa;
      }
    </style>
  </head>
  <body>
    <div id="dropZone"
        ondrop="drop(event)"
        ondragover="allowDrop(event)">
    </div>
    <br>
    <div id="ball"
        draggable="true"
        ondragstart="drag(event)"></div>
    <script>
      function allowDrop(ev) {
        ev.preventDefault();
      }
      function drag(ev) {
        ev.dataTransfer.setData("text", ev.target.id);
      }
      function drop(ev) {
        ev.preventDefault();
        var data = ev.dataTransfer.getData("text");
        ev.target.appendChild(document.getElementById(data));
      }
    </script>
  </body>
</html>
```

The output of the code looks like following screenshot before dragging with both the element are in there original position.

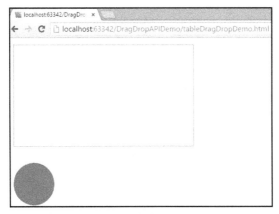

The output of the code looks like following screenshot after dragging and dropping the draggable element to the container.

Chapter 15 App Cache API

Q. What is app cache? What are the benefits of using app cache API in a web application?
ANSWER
App cache API is the new feature provided by the HTML5.This API power up a web application working without an internet connection. The most important benefits by this API are listed below:-

- **Speed**: Like all other cache it increases the speed of accessing the page content.

- **Offline browsing**: It increases the usability of application as it can be accessed without internet.

- **Reduced load**: As the content and data is now cache in the browser the load of the application is reduced form the server.

Few network calls: As most of reusable content is present in app cache it this reduces the no of network call to the server.

Q. How to enable application cache in an html file?
ANSWER
To enable application cache in a HTML file we need to have **manifest** attribute in **<HTML>** element containing the name of the **appcache** file. The syntax of declaring application cache in HTML file is as follows.

```
<!DOCTYPE HTML>
<html manifest="filename.appcache">
</html>
```

Q. What is the media type of appcache file?
ANSWER
A manifest file needs to have **text/cache-manifest** media type.

Q. What are the 3 different section of manifest file?

A manifest file has 3 different sections. These 3 different sections are as follows.

- **CACHE MANIFEST**: Files listed under this header will be cached after they are downloaded for the first time.
- **NETWORK**: Files listed under this header require a connection to the server, and will never be cached.
- **FALLBACK**: Files listed under this header specifies fallback pages if a page is inaccessible.

Q. What is NETWORK section?

NETWORK is one of the sections in manifest file. The file name listed in the NETWORK section is never cached locally. The following code shows a sample of NETWORK section.

```
NETWORK:
login.html
```

Q. What is FALLBACK section?

FALLBACK is one of the sections in manifest file. In this section we can mention the **file** name which will be called when application is offline. The following code shows a sample of FALLBACK section.

```
FALLBACK:
/html/ /offline.html
```

Q. What is CACHE MANIFEST section?

CACHE MANIFEST is one of the sections in manifest file. The file names mentioned in this section is cached locally. The following code shows a sample of CACHE MANIFEST section.

/style.css
/favicon.gif
/app.js

Q. How to view app cache detail in chrome browser?

We can view the app cache content like what it is caching, size and time etc. using the following link in chrome browser.

chrome://appcache-internals/.

The following screenshot shows the appcache internal for my browser.

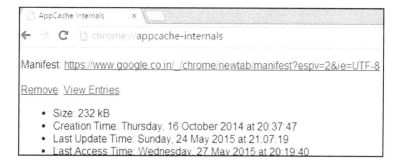

Q. How to detect the support of browser for appcache?

We can detect the support of appcache by checking the existence of **applicationCache** in **window** object. We can use javascript if statement which checks the truth value of **window.applicationCache** object. The following screenshot shows the chrome console detecting applicationCache object.

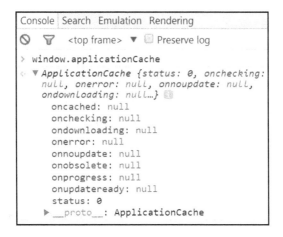

Q. How to update the appcache manually?

ANSWER

We can update the cache by doing hard reload to the browser. We can also call **swapCache()** method to programmatically update the cache.

Chapter 16 Server Sent Events

Q. What is Server Side Events (SSE)?
ANSWER
HTML5 provides server side events feature by which a web page gets the update from the server automatically. A great example of this feature is Facebook notification or Google + updates.

Q. What is the content type of the server sent response?
ANSWER
The content type of the server response is "**text/event-stream**" for the "**Content-Type**" header.

Q. How to create an event source for listening to server updates?
ANSWER
An event source can be created by instantiating the object of **EventSource** class with a server path. The syntax for creating an event source is listed below.

    var source = new EventSource("<URL to Server>");

Q. What are the event types is fired by an EventSource?
ANSWER
An EventSource fires 3 different events. Callback methods can be attached to the source for listening to these events. These event types are listed below.

- **onopen**: This event is fired when the server open the connection to the browser.
- **onmessage**: This event is fired when server produces the new output to the stream.
- **onerror**: This event is fired when an error occurs by some means.

Q. How to close an event stream?

The event stream can be closed using **close()** method.

Q. What is the format of event stream?
The event stream is a simple stream of text data, which must be encoded using **UTF-8**. Each message is separated by a pair of newline characters. A colon as the first character of a line is, in essence, a comment, and is ignored.

Chapter 17 Miscellaneous Questions

Q. What is strict mode?

ANSWER

Strict mode is a new directive in new ECMA 5 JavaScript specification. It is used for secure JavaScript coding. It eliminates some JavaScript silent errors by changing them to throw errors.

The syntax of writing strict mode is below expression.

"use strict"

Below code shows the use of strict mode inside a function.

```
function sayHello(){
    "use strict";
    myName = "Sandeep";
}
sayHello();
```

The following screenshot shows the error produces by using an undeclared variable inside the **sayHello()** method.

Q. List out some of the conditions that are not allowed in strict mode?

Find the list of the conditions that are not allowed in ECMA5 strict mode in below:-

- Using a variable without declaring is not allowed.
- Deleting a variable, a function, or an argument is not allowed.
- Defining a property more than once is not allowed.
- Duplicating a parameter name is not allowed.
- Octal numeric literals and escape characters are not allowed.
- Writing to a read-only property is not allowed.
- Deleting an undeletable property is not allowed.
- The string "eval" cannot be used as a variable.
- The string "arguments" cannot be used as a variable.
- The with statement is not allowed.
- Future reserved keywords are not allowed.

Q. What is the output of 0.1+0.2 produces in the console and why?

ANSWER

JavaScript math library follows IEEE 754 standards for math. IEEE 754 standards use 64 bit representation for a floating point number. This causes a problem while evaluating the 0.1 + 0.2 expression. Below screenshot shows the Firebug console for this expression.

```
Clear Persist Profile   Run Clear Copy Pretty Print Histo
var sum = 0.1 +        1 var sum = 0.1 + 0.2;
0.2;                   2 console.log(sum);
console.log(sum);
0.30000000000000004
```

JavaScript internally converts the 0.1 to 16 precision which becomes 0.1000000000000000 and then 0.2 gets added and becomes 0.30000000000000004. Below screenshot shows this demonstration in JavaScript code.

```
Console ▾ HTML CSS Script DOM Net Cookies Page Speed Typography
Clear Persist Profile  All Errors Warnir Run Clear Copy Pretty Print  History
var num1 = 0.1.toPrecision(16)         1 var num1 = 0.1.toPrecision(16)
num2 = 0.2; co...e.log(num1);          2       num2 = 0.2;
console.log(parseFloat(num1)+num2);    3 console.log(num1);
  0.1000000000000000                   4 console.log(parseFloat(num1)+num2);
  0.30000000000000004
```

Q. How to resolve the issue 0.1+0.2 = 0.30000000000000004 and produce 0.1+0.2 = 03?

ANSWER

This issue can be resolved by using to toFixed(1) method to this expression. toFixed() method converts a number to the specified decimal points. Below screenshot shows the use of toFixed() method to produce the correct output which is 0.3.

```
Console ▾ HTML CSS Script DOM Net Cookies Page Speed Typography
Clear Persist Profile  All Errors Run Clear Copy Pretty Print  History
var sum = 0.1+0.2;               1 var sum = 0.1+0.2;
console.log(sum);               2 console.log(sum);
console.log(sum.toFixed(1));    3 console.log(sum.toFixed(1));
  0.30000000000000004
  0.3
```

Q. What will be the output of the below code and why?

```
(function(){
  var a = b = 3;
})();
console.log(typeof a);
console.log(typeof b);
```

ANSWER

The above code will print undefined and Number in the console. Below screenshot shows the output of the above code in the Firebug console.

```
⚡ < > ≡  Console ▾  HTML  CSS  Script  DOM  Net  Cookies

↳  Clear  Persist  Profile  Run  Clear  Copy  Pretty Print  History

(function () {      var    1  (function () {
a = b = 3; }) ();          2     var a = b = 3;
console.log(typeof         3  }) ();
a);                        4  console.log(typeof a);
console.log(typeof         5  console.log(typeof b);
b);

  undefined
  number
```

JavaScript treats the above code as below screenshot. From the below code it is clear that variable **a** is in local scope of the function and be is treated as **this.b** . The current reference this represents the **window** object.

Q. What will be the output of the below code and why?

console.log(1+2+4);

ANSWER

The output of the above code is 7 as the parameters are all numbers. Below screenshot shows the output of the above code in a chrome console.

```
Q  ▯    Elements   Network   »          ⟩≡  ⚙  ▭  ×

◎  ▽    <top frame> ▼  ☐ Preserve log

> console.log(1+2+4);
  7                                          VM916:2
```

Q. Explain Hoisting in JavaScript?

ANSWER

Hoisting is JavaScript's default behavior of moving declarations to the top. In other words, a variable can be used before it has been declared. Let's understand hoisting using these following examples.

Example 1:

The following code has a **display()** method which prints the value of a in the console.

```
function display(){
  console.log(a);
}
display();
```

The output of the preceding code will be a **reference** error as we have not defined the variable. The following screenshot shows the output of the preceding code.

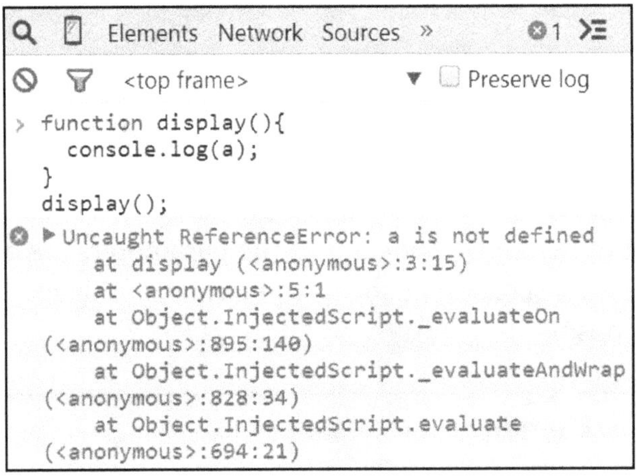

Example 2:

The following code has a **display()** method which prints the value of a in the console.

```
function display(){
  var a;
  console.log("Output: "+a);
}
display();
```

The output of the preceding code will be undefined as we have defined the variable but not assigned any value. The following screenshot shows the output of the preceding code.

```
Q  🔲  Elements  Network  Sources  Timeline  »   ⟫≡
◎  ▽   <top frame>              ▼ ☐ Preserve log
> function display(){
      var a;
      console.log("Output: "+a);
   }
   display();
   Output: undefined
```

Example 3:

The following code has a **display()** method which prints the value of a in the console.

```
function display(){
 console.log("Output: "+a);
 var a;
}
display();
```

The output of the preceding code will be undefined as we have defined the variable but not assigned any value. Example 2 and Example 3 has same output. It means the variable declaration is moved to the top. The following screenshot shows the output of the preceding code.

```
Q  🔲  Elements  Network  Sources  Timeline  »   ⟫≡
◎  ▽   <top frame>              ▼ ☐ Preserve log
> function display(){
      console.log("Output: "+a);
      var a;
   }
   display();
   Output: undefined
```

About The Author

Sandeep Kumar Patel is a senior web developer and founder of www.tutorialsavvy.com, a widely- read programming blog since 2012. He has more than five years of experience in object-oriented JavaScript and JSON-based web applications development. He is GATE-2005 Information Technology (IT) qualified and has a Master's degree from VIT University, Vellore.

You can know more about him from his

-LinkedIn profile (http://www.linkedin.com/in/techblogger).

-He has received the Dzone Most Valuable Blogger (MVB) award for technical publications related to web technologies. His article can be viewed at http://www.dzone.com/users/sandeepgiet.

-He has also received the Java Code Geek (JCG) badge for a technical article published in JCG. His article can be viewed at http://www.javacodegeeks.com/author/sandeep-kumar-patel/.

-Author of "Instant GSON" for Packt publication,

http://www.packtpub.com/create-json-data-java-objects-implement-with-gson-library/book

Questions or comments? E-mail me at sandeeppateltech@gmail.com or find me on the following social networks:-

-Facebook Page:

http://www.facebook.com/SandeepTechTutorials .

-Tutorial Blog: http://www.tutorialsavvy.com

One Last Thing...

When you turn the page, Kindle will give you the opportunity to rate this book and share your thoughts on Facebook and Twitter. If you believe the book is worth sharing, please would you take a few seconds to let your friends know about it? If it turns out to make a difference in their professional lives, they'll be forever grateful to you, as will I.

All the best,
Sandeep Kumar Patel.